BYZANTINE
FRESCOES

BYZANTINE FRESCOES

from Yugoslav Churches

INTRODUCTION BY
DAVID TALBOT RICE

A MENTOR-UNESCO ART BOOK

PUBLISHED BY
THE NEW AMERICAN LIBRARY OF WORLD LITERATURE, INC.
BY ARRANGEMENT WITH UNESCO

FIRST PRINTING, MAY, 1963

MENTOR TRADEMARK REG. U. S. PAT. OFF. AND FOREIGN COUNTRIES
REGISTERED TRADEMARK—MARCA REGISTRADA

MENTOR-UNESCO ART BOOKS ARE PUBLISHED BY
THE NEW AMERICAN LIBRARY OF WORLD LITERATURE, INC.
501 MADISON AVENUE, NEW YORK 22, NEW YORK

PRINTED IN ITALY BY AMILCARE PIZZI S.P.A., MILANO

The title of this book is perhaps somewhat misleading, for it is only the painting of the eastern half of what is today Yugoslavia, namely the provinces of Serbia and Macedonia, that is dealt with here. The mountains of Montenegro and Bosnia have always constituted a more effective barrier than the Adriatic Sea, and the lands to the east of them have for centuries formed part of the Byzantine cultural sphere while the coastlands to the west have been more closely linked with Italy. It is, then, the painting of Macedonia and Serbia that is our concern, and for the sake of convenience the subject may be considered under three principal headings: first, that done when both these provinces formed a part of the great Byzantine Empire with its capital at Constantinople; second that done after the Southern Slavs — for that is the meaning of the word "Yugoslavia" — had achieved independence, but when Byzantine influence was still much to the fore; and third, that done after about 1350, when links both with East and West had to a great extent been severed and when the painters were forced to draw on local resources rather than to look elsewhere for inspiration.

Of these periods, the paintings done during the first are perhaps the most monumental and impressive, those of the second perhaps the most attractive and successful artistically, while those of the third, though often interesting historically and iconographically and at times redolent of considerable charm, were more restricted and on the whole less important from the aesthetic point of view.

5

Most of the work of all these periods takes the form of wall-painting; mosaic, perhaps the most characteristic Byzantine art, is not represented in Yugoslavia. Painted panels were doubtless important from about 1200 onward, but not many dating from before about 1300 have survived. All the art, broadly speaking, belongs to the Byzantine family; that is to say, it follows a set iconography, is concerned with wholly Christian themes, and is intended for church decoration. We know practically nothing about secular art in Yugoslavia at this time, and very little about Byzantine secular art in general. But this does not mean that the work was unduly limited in character, or that it was lacking in expression, for much of it was of very high quality and great beauty, even if the artist was never permitted the same personal freedom as he was in the Western world; and all of it was profoundly spiritual. The artists worked, indeed, for the greater glory of God, not for themselves, and the great sincerity that such an approach entails served to redeem the lack of finish that is at times apparent. The basic spirituality of approach that characterizes the work is surely no bad thing as a driving force toward the production of great art.

Unfortunately, not many monuments of the first period survive, for this early work was often destroyed to make way for more up-to-date decorations at subsequent dates. But there are a number of paintings in small churches distributed over Macedonia that are to be dated before the last quarter of the twelfth century, when the area won its independence from Byzantine overlordship; most notable are those at Vodoca (probably eleventh century), at Djurdjevi Stupovi (c. 1168), at Kurbinovo (c. 1191), and at Monastir near Prilep; the paintings at Kurbinovo, though in some ways rather primitive, nevertheless have a humanism and intimacy of approach unusual at this early period. But more important are the decorations of two larger and richer churches, one at Ochrid and the other at Nerezi, near Skoplje, both of which are in a more metropolitan style. The paintings in the first date from

The Church of Nerezi, 1164.

shortly before 1050; those in the second from 1164. Both were recovered from below layers of subsequent plaster and repaint in the years between the wars; the work of cleaning and restoration at Ochrid has only recently been completed.

The paintings at Ochrid adorn the church of Saint Sophia, originally a three-aisled cruciform building with a dome, of quite considerable size (Plates 1 to 7). The paintings are of very high quality indeed. They comprise a number of Old Testament and New Testament scenes, portraits of saints, a striking frieze of angels, a moving rendering of the Forty Martyrs, an impressive *Ascension* on the roof of the apse, and a great *Dormition of the Virgin* on the west wall. This served as a prototype for subsequent renderings of the scene elsewhere, for it was one that was to become very popular in Yugoslavia, where it was elaborated in a way hardly paralleled in Byzantine Greece. In Saint Sophia the rendering is comparatively simple, even austere, but the figure of Christ, who stands behind the bier to receive the Virgin's soul, is of great beauty; it was never surpassed in the whole of Byzantine art. His face is painted more subtly and with greater expression than it is, for instance, in the *Ascension* (Plate 1), and would seem to be by a different, though no doubt contemporary, hand. But if some of the other figures lack the tenderness of expression of the Christ in the *Dormition*, all have grandeur and dignity — this is well exemplified in the figures of Apostles in the *Ascension* or in those of the Fathers of the Church on the lower registers of the walls — and some show a vividness of expression and liveliness of movement that is equaled only in some of the miniature paintings of the age, like those of the Psalter in the British Museum, which was done in the Monastery of Studion at Constantinople in 1066; the scene of the *Sacrifice of Abraham* at Saint Sophia in Ochrid may be cited (Plate 4).

It is however perhaps the grandeur of the compositions and dignity of the figures that most distinguish this series of paintings, together with the beauty of the coloring. This too is to be classed as impressive rather than captivating, with its deep greens, purples, and blues, but the contrasts are supremely effective, and if at first glance the tones seem somewhat somber and mournful, closer acquaintance proves their worth. "Bright colors captivate the crowd, but the true artist seeks to delight the judicious," wrote Leonardo da Vinci. The coloring of the wall-paintings of Saint Sophia at Ochrid would certainly not have displeased him.

Few Byzantine wall-paintings of this age have survived and the closest parallels to those in Saint Sophia at Ochrid that we have are to be found in the great Byzantine mosaic decorations of the eleventh century, notably that of Saint Sophia at Kiev (1037-61), where the same rather monumental style is to the fore; the Kiev mosaics were done in part by Byzantine craftsmen who traveled from Constantinople for the purpose, and the Ochrid paintings are similarly to be attributed in part to Greek craftsmen, but whether they came from the capital or from Salonica, which was almost equally important as a center of artistic production, it is hard to say. In any case there is little that one would term provincial about the paintings at Ochrid; they must, in fact, be counted as one of the major monuments of mid-Byzantine art that have come down to us.

The next important group of paintings that survives on Yugoslav soil is in the little church of Nerezi near Skoplje (Plates 8 to 10). They were done in 1164, under the patronage of a member of the Byzantine ruling family, the Comneni, and in this case there is good reason to believe that the artist was brought from Constantinople. But if the Ochrid paintings represent the grand manner of the Macedonian age of Byzantine art, those at Nerezi are in a distinct style and herald the art of the age that was to come, which is generally known as the Byzantine Renaissance or the Byzantine Revival. They are indeed extremely progressive works and are quite distinct both from most other Byzantine manifestations of twelfth-century date and from certain other

Studenica, Church of Milutin. Dormition of the Virgin.
Detail: Apostles behind the open sarcophagus. (See Plate 22).

The Monastery of Dečani, 1327-1335.

paintings in Macedonia which are wholly provincial, such as those in the church of Saint George at Kurbinovo, mentioned above, and those of Saint Nicholas Varos at Prilep.

The essential feature of the work at Nerezi, apart from its quality, is the new humanism and greater delicacy of approach. The Saint Sophia paintings were grand and impressive; those at Nerezi are intimate and tender. Though the conventions are those of Byzantine art as a whole, with its rigid iconography, severely stressed highlights, angular modeling and linear conventions in the faces, greatly elongated figures, and so forth, the facial expressions are nevertheless personal, the figures are those of individuals, and the scenes tell by the sympathy and human understanding of their rendering. In the *Deposition*, for example (Plate 8), the Virgin is wholly the Mother, embracing the body of her beloved Son, while the profundity of Nicodemus's grief could hardly have been more effectively rendered, though there is no undue exaggeration or overstressing of emotion. The new outlook that we see here is also characteristic of certain other works of the age, notably the lovely icon known as *Our Lady of Vladimir*, painted at Constantinople around 1130 and now in the Tretyakov Gallery at Moscow. But this intimate style was not characteristic of the age as a whole, and it would seem to have been developed at Constantinople alongside a more formal rather cold, essentially linear manner, which we see for instance in the enamels of the age or in the mosaic known as the John panel in Saint Sophia at Constantinople, which dates from about 1118. Both of these styles apparently spread from the capital to other centers, and both exercised their influence in Macedonia, the one at Nerezi, the other in a few smaller places, mostly in the mountains; the style even penetrated as far west as Dalmatia, for the paintings of the church of Saint Chrysogonus at Zadar are in the Comnene linear manner, whereas most of the work to the west of the mountains shows Latin rather than Greek relationships.

In the Byzantine world, artists seem to have been, in the main, conservative and the same was true of Macedonia, for the Comnene linear style apparently dominated there through much of the thirteenth century. The sharply accentuated and rather dramatic character that was to become a dominant feature of Macedonian painting in the later thirteenth and fourteenth centuries was no doubt the result of a blend of the two outlooks, the humanism of the one being blended with the angularity of the other to produce the new dramatic Macedonian manner, which was later to become characteristic of a distinct Macedonian school. The history of that school became extremely important from just before 1300, when a number of outstanding painters were working both in the Slav and the Greek portions of the land we know as Macedonia. Throughout the thirteenth century, however, it was not there but in Serbia, to the north, that the most important work was done, and we must move to that area in order to follow up the story in chronological sequence.

The story of Serbian painting begins in the territory of Raška, where the early Serbian Tsars built and endowed a series of important monasteries and where most of them were subsequently buried. The earliest paintings that we have are those in the church of Saint George at Ras, but they stand somewhat apart. More typical are the thirteenth-century paintings at Studenica, which already show many of the features most characteristic of the Raška school. But the most progressive and interesting work of the age is probably that in the narthex of the church at Mileševa (c. 1135). This was followed by work in the church of the Mother of God (1208-09) and that of Saint Nicholas (end of thirteenth century) at Studenica, at Žiča (1219-35), in the central church at Peć (c. 1250), at Morača (1252), at Gradać (1270), at Arilje (c. 1296) and at Sopoćani (1260). Much of this is distinctive; that at Mileševa and Sopoćani is of especially high quality.

The paintings at Mileševa are perhaps the best (Plates

13

11 to 13). They are of course in the main Byzantine, but new ideas have brought about changes in iconography, and the style is personal and individual. The scene of the *Resurrection* (Plate 12), for instance, still follows a Byzantine tradition in that it is rendered allegorically by showing the empty tomb with the angel beside it, and not, as in the West, by an attempt to depict the event realistically, but the tomb is reduced in size and so changed, and the angel so enlarged, that there is little similarity to any Byzantine prototype. It is, however, the style and the actual handling that are most distinctive. The linear manner of some Comnene art, the exaggerated use of highlights, and the elongated proportions of the figures have been abandoned in favor of a solider manner where the features are modeled in mass and the faces are built up in dark tones by the superposition of one color above another, rather than by the addition of white highlights on the surface. A comparison of the rendering of the Virgin in the *Annunciation* (Plate 11) or the Angel in the *Resurrection* (Plate 12) at Mileševa with that of Saint Simeon at Nerezi (Plate 10) serves to illustrate this quite clearly. The angel is painted in a style suggestive of the late antique, as we see it, for example, in the eighth-century paintings in Santa Maria Antiqua at Rome. The change of manner appears even more striking if we look at one of the donor portraits like that of King Vladislav (Plate 13). It is true that in Byzantine art the ascetic appearance of the saintly, prophetic, or divine portraits never characterized the depictions of living or recently deceased human beings, but even so the donors at Mileševa are painted in a three-dimensional, roundly modeled style, which in many ways savors of the secular art of the West rather than of the religious art of Byzantium. Mileševa is the most westerly of the monasteries, being situated on the fringe of Bosnia, and the changes are perhaps to be attributed to Western influence; Radojčić has even compared some of the paintings there to those of Giunta Pisano. But similar hints of the West are to be seen elsewhere; they

14

Bogorodica Ljeviška at Prizren, 1307-1309.

are most marked in stone sculptures of a slightly earlier date like those above the door between the narthex and the church in the monastery of Studenica.

This progressive, more fully modeled, style appears again at Sopoćani (Plates 14 to 17), but the experimental stage of Mileševa has been passed and a new tranquillity, a new dignity, serves to distinguish this as the most complete and most perfect monument of Serbian painting. The classical manner which we noted in the angel at Mileševa (Plate 12) has become dominant over the linear Comnene style, but the colors are richer and more varied than ever before; the details of the backgrounds are fuller and more interesting and the modeling more pronounced. It is here that Serbian painting is to be seen at its best, and though some monuments are more complete, others more extensive, and others more elaborate, none is more beautiful. The paintings of Mileševa and Sopoćani are indeed works of really outstanding quality.

Two more thirteenth-century decorations must be mentioned, that of the central church at Peć, of about 1230, and that at Morača. The former is archaic and rather ascetic, features made the more obvious by the fact that the backgrounds are dark blue, almost black, whereas at Mileševa and Sopoćani they are yellow or even gold, in imitation of mosaics. The paintings at Morača are more truly Serbian, but they lack the beauty and mastery of the best of the work at Sopoćani.

If the years around 1250 saw the first flowering of the Serbian school proper, those around 1300 saw the fulfillment of earlier promise in both Serbia and Macedonia in the decoration of a whole series of churches from Ochrid in the south to Žiča in the north. A particular group of painters, with a man who called himself Astrapas at their head, and with his pupils Michael and Eutychios following after, executed and in some cases signed decorations in the Perebleptos (Saint Clement) at Ochrid (1295), at Arilje (1296), at Prizren (1309), at Žiča (1310), in the church of Saint Nikitas near Skoplje (1310), at Staro-Nagoricino (1317) and at Gračanica (1321). The name of Michael has also recently been discovered in connection with paintings at Lesnovo. Many other paintings are in the same style, though not actually signed. The debt to the earlier artists who worked at Mileševa and Sopoćani is apparent in all this work, but contacts with the Byzantine world had been renewed and the Western elements that were apparent at Mileševa had proved to be of an ephemeral nature, so that it is not easy to tell some of these works from those of contemporary artists on the Greek side of the border. Indeed, the principal Greek city of the region, Salonica, played an important part in the development of the Macedonian school; so far as Yugoslavia was concerned it was, from about 1250, just as important a center of influence as Constantinople itself. Political events no doubt had their role to play in bringing about this state of affairs, for when the earlier paintings of Serbia were being done, Constantinople was still under the domination of the Latins (1204-61) and was hardly in a position to exercise any influence. But the years around 1300, when Astrapas and his followers were painting, was an age of particular brilliance in the Byzantine world as a whole, for it was then that the superb mosaics and wall-paintings in the church now known as Kariye Camii at Constantinople were set up and work which was well-nigh as outstanding was also being done in other churches at the capital, in the Holy Apostles and elsewhere at Salonica, and probably in other churches in Greece too. It is the period we know as the Byzantine Renaissance and corresponds exactly in date to the age of Giotto and Duccio in Italy.

There must have been a great deal of artistic interchange at this time. The mosaics of the Holy Apostles at Salonica, done in 1312, are closely akin to those of Kariye Camii; there were close links between Salonica and Macedonia, and there were probably also direct contacts between Macedonia and Constantinople. Astrapas, Michael, and Eutychios were certainly developing a local style of their own, and it is to be seen in some of the icons of this age as well as in the wall-paintings, but other icons,

Saint Sophia at Ochrid, eleventh century.

18

The Church of the Ascension, Mileševa, 1230-1237.

notably an outstandingly lovely one with the *Virgin and Child* on one side and the *Annunciation* on the other, from the Church of Saint Clement at Ochrid, now at Skoplje, were painted in Constantinople. Other icons from the same church, on the other hand, are of local workmanship, and some of them many actually be by painters Michael and Eutychios, who worked on the wall-paintings there in 1296.

Most of these paintings are of quality, even if they lack something of the aspiring brilliance of the earlier work. But one series stands out especially, namely that in the church of the Mother of God, Ljeviska, at Prizren (Plates 18 and 19). It may be that this is so to some extent because of the freshness and brilliance of the color, for the church was turned into a mosque by the Turks and the paintings were plastered over, to be uncovered only a few years ago, whereas those elsewhere have either been blackened by smoke or have been subjected for long periods to the action of wind and rain. But even allowing for this, there is something about the Prizren paintings that distinguishes them artistically, for they have a freshness and brilliance that is unique. Perhaps they alone of all the works are to be assigned to Astrapas, while the others were to a greater degree due to the hands of his followers, Michael, Eutychios, and others, whose names we do not know. The church too perhaps presented greater possibilities, for it was a comparatively large basilica with considerable areas of open wall space, whereas the majority of the buildings of the period were smaller, and more confined.

As the fourteenth century progressed, tall buildings with rather complicated ground plans and numerous narrow arches and small vaults became characteristic — the monastery church of Gračanica (Plates 23 and 24) is the most outstanding of them. The painters knew how to adapt their style to these buildings, and it can safely be said that at no other time in the history of art have interior decorations been so satisfactorily conceived in relation to the architecture. But the areas to be decorated were often of awkward shape and space was usually confined, so that it is not surprising that the grandeur of the early work at times gave place to a somewhat finicky style. The artist tended to become somewhat overpreoccupied with the business of storytelling at the cost of composition and glory. And this effect was intensified by the development of the habit of writing up not only the titles of the scenes, but also the names of the protagonists and sometimes even words of the texts that were illustrated. An example of this tendency is to be seen at Dečani (Plate 25), where the church is decorated with no fewer than twenty cycles, each with numerous scenes; in that of the *Passion* alone there are forty-three, in that of *Genesis* forty-six, and in that of the *Last Judgment* twenty-six. With such profusion, grandeur of style or great significance of interpretation is hardly to be expected, even if the church is a mine of interest to the student of iconography.

At about this time, primarily for theological and political reasons, contacts with Constantinople seem to have been broken off, and with the middle of the century art tended to become somewhat provincial. But though contacts with Constantinople were probably resumed when the Serbian and Greek churches were reconciled in 1375, the capital was no longer the vital source that it had been, and there was not alive in Serbia the spirit that had produced work of such outstanding quality a century earlier. Yet some of this art, even if it was provincial, deserves careful attention, for Macedonia was far from being a sterile center, and masters from there spread into Serbia from about 1370 and produced work which was by no means lacking in vigor. There was a flourishing school at Prilep and a series of paintings in the monastery of Saint Andrew on the Treska River, done in 1389, are truly beautiful. And work of great brilliance, even if it is sometimes closer to "peasant" than to "fine" art, was also often done in the monasteries; of these, the wall-paintings of the monastery of Markos (1370-75) are perhaps the most interesting. Some of the figures show a keenness of observation and stressing of character that is almost in the realm of caricature. The irascible and violent monks who made the lives of the novices so intolerable, and who are described in legendaries of the fourteenth century, seem to have come alive on the walls. These tendencies may have been to some extent the result of Western influence, for they are quite foreign to Byzantine art and do not appear in Greece.

A lessening of Byzantine influence in Serbia was also brought about by historical events, for in the second half of the fourteenth century Macedonia was lost, and Serbian power was forced to concentrate in the north in the Morava Valley, and a distinct "Morava" school of painting developed. The region was a secluded one and contacts with the outside world had not been established previously. As a result, greater stress came to be set on the beauty of the inner life, and, as a sort of escapism from the uncertainty of outside events, art took on a somewhat sentimental garb. The decorations of the age, at Ravanica (c. 1377), Sisojevac (end of fourteenth century), Ljubostinja (end of fourteenth century), Kalenic (1413-17), Rudenica (1403-10) and Resava, also called Manasija, (1407-18) have undoubted charm, even if the paintings are less profound that those of earlier date. Paintings in the dome at Manasija are probably the finest of the group (Plates 26 to 28). These works represent the last important phase of painting in Yugoslavia. But it was a phase that was short-lived, for the empire fell to the Turks around 1453, and little of real consequence was done after that date.

What has been written above has been mainly on the subject of wall-paintings, the importance of many of which in the history of Byzantine art can hardly be exaggerated; they also have a not inconsiderable part to play in the story of European art of the time as a whole. But though the wall-paintings constitute the most important aspect of our study, a word must also be said about the panel paintings, the icons as they are usually called in the Orthodox world, for they too were important, and a

The Church of Sopoćani, 1260.

distinctive South Slav style was as fully developed in icon painting as it was in wall-painting. Happily, quite large numbers of icons of the fourteenth century survive, more particularly from the church of Saint Clement at Ochrid; most of them are now in the museum at Skoplje. Some are perhaps to be attributed to the painters Michael and Eutychios, who worked on the wall-paintings in the same church. It is hardly possible at present to tell the work of one of these masters from that of the other, but the icons as a whole are characterized by a mat texture and by a palette which is quite distinct from that usual in Byzantine and Greek icons of the period. And the same style and the same range of palette seem to characterize icons from other Serbian churches that are now preserved in the museums of Belgrade and Skoplje; some of the finest of all are preserved in the Serbian monastery of Chilandari on Mount Athos. These panel paintings still remain but little known in the West, but many of them are things of great beauty and our galleries would be the richer if they were to possess examples of the school.

ILLUSTRATIONS

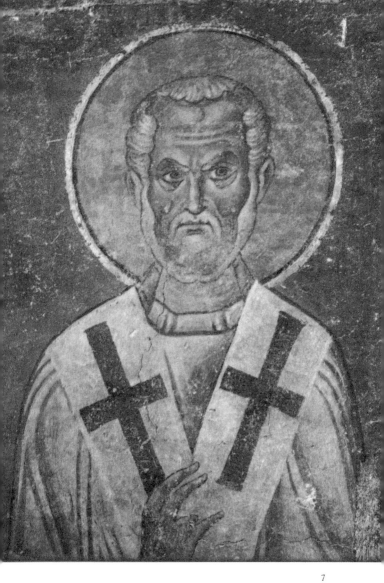

23

ΙΣ ΧΣ

ϹΟΔΟΜ
ЄΜΓΡΙϹΜΟϹ

ΑΚΗΠ

ΖΟΡΟ
ΒΑΒЄΛ

BIBLIOGRAPHY

LATER BYZANTINE PAINTING:

GRABAR, A., *La peinture byzantine*, Skira, Genève, 1953.

LAZAREV, V. N., *Istorja vizantiskoj zivopisi* (History of Byzantine Painting), Moskva, 1947-1948.

RICE, D. TALBOT, *Byzantine Art*, London, 1954.

YUGOSLAV ART:

CVETKOV, M., *Raška*, Parts I to III, Beograd, 1939. (Text in Serbo-Croat, English, French and German).

DJURIĆ, V. J., *Icônes de Yougoslavie*, Beograd, 1961.

KASANIN, M., *L'Art yougoslave*, Beograd, 1939.

MILLET, G., *Recherches sur l'iconographie de l'Evangile*, Paris, 1917.

MILLET, G., *La Peinture du moyen âge en Yougoslavie* (albums présentés par A. Frolow). I and II, Paris, 1954 and 1957.

OKUNEV, N. L., *Monumenta artis serbicae*. Vols. I to IV, Praha, 1928-1932. (Brief text in French and German).

PETKOVIĆ, V. R. *La Peinture serbe au moyen âge*, Vols. I and II, Beograd, 1930.

RADOJĆIĆ, S., *Majstori starog srpskog slikarstva* (The Masters of Early Serbian Painting), Beograd, 1955. (Text in Serbo-Croat - brief summary in French).

RADOJĆIĆ, S., *Icônes de Serbie et de Macédoine*, Beograd, 1961.

RADOJĆIĆ, S. & RICE, D. TALBOT, *Yugoslavia - Mediaeval Frescoes*, Unesco World Art Series, Paris, 1955.

VERCORS, "L'Art médiéval yougoslave", *Art et Style*, Vol. XV, Paris, 1950.

CONTENTS

The color photography for the illustrations in this book was carried out by a special Unesco mission which visited Yugoslavia for this purpose and to collect the necessary documentation. This mission worked in close conjunction with the governmental authorities of Yugoslavia and Unesco wishes to express its appreciation to all those who collaborated in this work.

* * *

CONTENTS

Continued overleaf ▶

CONTENTS